T0380719

ABOUT THE AUTHOR

Mike is the owner of IntegrityWorks Coaching – an integrity-driven coaching, training and consulting company focused on planned and purposeful growth for individuals, teams and organizations, with a specific focus on sales, leadership, communication and team development. Mike is an Authorized Partner & Facilitator in Everything DiSC and The Five Behaviors of a Cohesive Team.

Mike is also the author of two books, 60 Second Time Out and 60 Second Leadership written to bring personal and professional development to sales and business leaders. Published in 4 countries, Mike's books have reached sales exceeding 75,000 copies worldwide.

Mike and his wife Amy have been married for over 34 years – committed to an exciting relationship centered in their faith and what Amy calls CPR (compromise, pursuit, and respect). Mike and Amy have three children and two grandchildren and plan nearly everything outside their careers around their family.

60 SECOND SUCCESS

TRANSFORM YOUR LIFE ONE THOUGHTFUL MINUTE AT A TIME

MIKE GREENE

WESTBOW
PRESS®
A DIVISION OF THOMAS NELSON
& ZONDERVAN

WestBow Press books may be ordered through booksellers or by contacting:

WestBow Press
A Division of Thomas Nelson & Zondervan
1663 Liberty Drive
Bloomington, IN 47403
www.westbowpress.com
844-714-3454

ISBN: 979-8-3850-2953-2 (sc)
ISBN: 979-8-3850-2954-9 (hc)
ISBN: 979-8-3850-2952-5 (e)

Library of Congress Control Number: 2024914528

Print information available on the last page.

WestBow Press rev. date: 02/03/2025

1

PATIENCE

Sometimes you need to slow down to go fast.
—Jeff Olson

IS ANYONE INTO meditation? I've tried, failed, and will likely try again. My wife shared with me a particularly impactful meditation that lasted five full minutes. It was a woman's voice. There were only four words repeated very slowly, over and over again. There ... is ...no ... rush.

Did you read that right? Take four beats in between each word. Wow! That's it! Talk about requiring patience! Can you imagine listening to "There ... is ... no ... rush" over and over for five minutes?

And that phrase has stuck with us ever since. We use it all the time, even sarcastically because we know the reality sometimes is "There is a rush!"

It really is helping me. Ever been in heavy traffic? There is no rush. Ever had someone cut you off? There is no rush. Ever been caught behind someone going slow in the passing lane, matching the right lane traffic so no one gets through? There is no rush. Seriously, the highways are the best training ground for patience, aren't they?

Did you know the Chinese bamboo tree doesn't grow for five years? You water it and take care of it for five years. And in the sixth year, over six weeks, it grows eighty feet! Clearly, for the bamboo tree, there was no rush.

What lessons can we learn from this? Stay the course with your exercise, career, marriage, faith, education, and investments. Unless a new course is absolutely necessary, stay the course.

As a former salesperson and still one in my own business, I've learned patience is the greatest virtue. As long as I'm swinging the bat with the right mechanics and attitude, I've learned there's a slight edge in motion. And if I stay the course, I'll eventually reach my destination. Tortoise and the hare anyone?

The next time you set out to do something great—exercising, quitting smoking, building wealth, raising kids, growing your marriage, and reading the Bible—as long as there is a purpose and a process, remember, there ... is ... no ... rush.

2 CHAPTER

1 PERCENT

If two men on the same job agree all the time, then one is useless. If they disagree all the time, then both are useless.
—DARRYL F. ZANUCK

BELIEFS DRIVE BEHAVIORS, just like goals do. Our beliefs tend to drive how we choose to see things and thereby create a heavy dose of influence as to why we are at odds with people who hold very different beliefs. We just see things differently, rooted in our upbringing, environment, experiences, and influences.

Presidential races are so much fun, or maybe not. Ever seen a Facebook post by one side that changes the opinion of someone on the other side? Doubt it. Ever see someone verbally attack another person who is diametrically opposed in their beliefs on some lighthearted stuff, like politics, religion, or climate change? Doubt it.

Our son, Mitchell, came home from work the other day and told us about an interesting conversation he had with his boss. He's a good guy, by the way. Both have high respect for each other. He and his boss were discussing something political. I don't know the specifics. Generally speaking, I think they are actually on the same side, though

Mitchell doesn't necessarily see himself on a particular side. He is more inclined to learn from people rather than debate people with different views. But I'm not so sure his boss shares the same open-minded attitude.

So seventeen-year-old Mitch respectfully offered this challenge to his boss: Go find someone with whom he is diametrically opposed in all major areas. If he's right-leaning, look for someone left-leaning. If he's a Democrat, look for a Republican. If he's pro-life, look for someone who considers themselves to be pro-choice. You get the picture.

Only that's not the challenge. It's pretty easy to find them. The challenge is to find the person, engage them, and genuinely search to find one thing, just one, they both share in common. Find the 1 percent and focus on that. Build a discussion around commonality. Maybe they both like animals, seafood, or perhaps a good microbrew. Perhaps they share a birthday, TV interests, or a sports team they follow. There's always something.

It was a great challenge. In fact, when he shared this with me, it made me think of a John Maxwell principle he offers in his book, *Winning with People*. It's called the 101% Principle. Find the 1 percent we agree on and give it 100 percent of our effort. Wow. Mitchell has never read a Maxwell book, yet he nailed a Maxwell leadership principle completely on his own.

Maybe we should accept this challenge. Find the 1 percent and build on that.

3

TWO-MINUTE DRILL

Each choice starts a behavior that over time becomes a habit.
—DARREN HARDY

"BEGINNING IS HALF-DONE." I heard Robert Schuller say this at a seminar I attended in Hershey, Pennsylvania, back in the 1990s. It's stuck with me ever since.

Once we engage in something, particularly something that is good but perhaps difficult, we cross the line of decision, the hardest of all lines to cross. Crossing is the beginning of execution.

So beginning is half-done. There's still the problem of beginning. That stops so many of us. Sometimes we cross that line, and other times we put it off, which leads us to the worst of all habits, inconsistency.

Years ago, I used motivation and accountability to maintain good habits. It worked to a point. But I recently started adding a different method, which I've found identified in a few books. It's called the two-minute drill. Simply put, it's a decision you make before you need to act. The decision is made to take a simple action toward a future decision, which begins your intended action or habit.

For example, I put on my exercise clothes first thing every morning. In fact, I make the decision to put them out the night before, making the next day's first decision easier. I put them on, knowing I'm not working out right away and maybe not at all. I've planned the time and activity, but not committed yet. But after a coffee and reading for thirty minutes, I'm more awake. And what do you know? I'm already wearing my workout clothes!

Beginning now is much easier because, in a way, I've already begun. So the action is also much easier to move into and accomplish.

You can do this with any goal. Set yourself up in advance. Do you need to eat better during the days in the office? Make your lunches every evening. Or better yet, prepare meals for the week on Sunday. I have a packed lunch every day I'm in the field, which is most days. My wife or I can make it easier each week by pulling all the consistent lunch items I have—veggies, fruit, and snacks. I gotta have some carbs! That way, less is required for daily prep. And eating out is almost never necessary unless I plan it. It's easy.

Another extension of this concept is to make the habit you want to eliminate or minimize difficult to engage. Less social media? Eliminate the apps. Less email distraction? Eliminate notifications. Need time to get in the zone? Remove your phone. Need to sleep better? Eliminate screen time one hour before bedtime or take the screen out of the room. Yes, I said it.

What can you apply the two-minute drill to?

20/20 FORESIGHT

It's said that a wise person learns from his mistakes.
A wiser one learns from others' mistakes. But the
wisest person of all learns from others' successes.
—JOHN MAXWELL

HAVE YOU EVER had 20/20 foresight? Many years ago, we were on our way to a conference amidst a nor'easter. This is long before GPS, so no shortcuts here.

As we were driving, traffic was building up ahead, and we had two options from which to choose. Both could work, but the one building up traffic was normally much faster. The longer option looked like the wise choice, but then we remembered a friend was going to the same conference and he was ahead of us. We called quickly and asked which way he went and how far ahead he was. It turns out he went the faster way that looked bad from our side. He said it was clear sailing about a mile up. We were off and running with 20/20 foresight from his 20/20 hindsight.

Why don't we do this more often? Aren't there always people further down the road we're on? We only have to choose the road: family, career, marriage, or health. Someone we know or have access to is much further down that road. Their hindsight can be our foresight.

Before my coaching and training business, I worked sixteen years for a printing company. I had sales experience but zero printing experience. What was my first move? I found out who had worked in my capacity before me. It was a guy named Blaine. He was highly successful and had moved on to work for a much large printer offering more opportunity.

I took him to lunch and asked dozens of questions, seeking his advice and ideas. It was a no-brainer. Some of what he said helped me realize my goals within this new venture.

The answers are out there. John Maxwell, way before he was famous as a leadership expert, would invest his vacation time by taking successful leaders out to dinner. One of them was John Wooden. Wooden became one of his greatest mentors and a significant factor in John Maxwell's leadership journey. I don't know how he got these meetings. Maybe he just asked!

Pick your road. Find someone significantly up ahead. And seek them out.

Who is your 20/20 foresight?

THREE SMARTS

You can make more friends in two months by becoming
interested in other people than you can in two years
by trying to get other people interested in you.
—DALE CARNEGIE

I'VE NEVER CONSIDERED myself super smart. Oh, I figure I'm smart enough to contribute and achieve in society. But in terms of book smarts, I just don't think I have it. I could be wrong about that, but not likely.

And I'm not overly practical either. When it comes to basic street smarts or, let's say, around the house, building, and fixing with your hands, once again, I'm not that smart! Oh, I can get by. I've been a homeowner for twenty-five years. Nothing has blown up yet! And I once even changed an oil filter. (I came out completely covered in oil afterward, but it was successfully changed.)

So I'm not an Einstein or a MacGyver. What's left? Well, in my opinion, there is one more intelligence: people smarts. Humbly, I think that's my ace. In life, it's pretty hard to avoid people. They're pretty much everywhere, in every transaction, activity, and endeavor.

Every day, we're interacting with each other, either making deposits or withdrawals from people's emotional bank accounts.

Sales is the obvious place of value in effectively dealing with people, yet truly sales, at some level, is a part of every human interaction. Get sincerely good at earning other people's trust, respect, and interest, and you're well on your way to success in life. Nail down the other two, Einstein and MacGyver, but if you miss the people part, you might be in trouble.

Still to this day, the inability or unwillingness to get along with others is one of the biggest reasons for job displacement. Nope, not competence or confidence in effectively dealing with people. If you miss that, you'll eventually lose.

So there you have three smarts: intellectual, practical, and people. I'm pretty sure I'm only one for three, but that's worked out pretty well so far.

The best-case scenario is to ace them all! But if you could only have one, what would you choose? For me, it's always been people smarts. That's a good thing.

**C
H
A
P
T
E
R**

A BAD FIT

When your values are clear to you, decisions become easier.
—ROY DISNEY

THERE WE WERE, rookie coaches, at an evening social event with other more seasoned coaches, trainers, staff, and spouses. I was talking with a few of the newbies, of which I was one, when the lead dog entered the room. This guy started this thing many years ago and built it into one of the most successful franchises of its kind. At least that was what I was told. I never really checked. Either way, this guy was a genius at how to build businesses by virtue of his own experience, his track record of helping others succeed, and the worldwide company he now owned.

It was pretty cool except for one small challenge: I didn't like him, not one little bit. While we were standing there chatting amongst ourselves, the big dog walked into the room and headed toward us. He didn't have much choice since we were right inside the door he used. He walked up and said something shallow, and I could not help but notice him looking over our heads. In all honesty, he was a pretty tall guy, but looking beyond us was pretty condescending.

What was he doing? Small, shallow, I-don't-care-who-you-are-or-what-your-story-is talk in order to buy time, look over our heads, and find someone he deemed important and far more worthy of a conversation. Then he was gone, off to someone or something seemingly better.

I hope you're getting the gist of what I'm sharing. If you are, you might have had similar experiences. Rude, arrogant, and condescending are not attributes I'm very fond of. Outwardly smart and successful as this guy was, he rubbed me so far the wrong way! I struggled from that point on with him being the leader of this entire gig. While many of my colleagues were the polar opposite of him, he was at the top, and that just did not sit well.

Our values are what we hold to be true and important in our lives. They are filters through which all decisions are made. If it fits the filter, keep moving forward; if not, run away. So I eventually ran, which was a good decision, one that led to my company today.

What are your top three to five values? Companies define these things often; some even live and execute through them consistently. But this is about you. What are your personal values? What filters do you use to evaluate careers, relationships, and difficult choices?

Having the right filters, or defined values, will lead us to make better decisions and live with fewer regrets. And that's a good way to live.

A MISSING VIRTUE

*Loyalty isn't grey. It's black and white. You're
either loyal completely, or not loyal at all.*
—SHARNAY

RECOGNITION AND ENCOURAGEMENT,
that's what's missing in the workplace, family, church, and everyday
interactions of life. No question. But I have another one, but not
better, worse, or by any means a substitute. In fact, this one is usually
a product of the others.

My mom was a high driver, a dominant and very direct type of
communicator. Those familiar with Everything DiSC would quickly
put her in the strong D quadrant of the DiSC assessment, which would
be correct. I even told her one day; she argued. Well, you get it.

Anyway, a high D has no less heart than anyone else, but sometimes
they rub others, especially their S (more sensitive) counterparts a little
the wrong way. If you know it, you can work with it. My wife knew it
and adjusted. It was tough when my mom would speak in a very direct,
matter-of-fact way with Amy, but she knew my mom's heart wasn't

accurately reflected in her initial perception of those words. My mom had heart and something else.

Case in point, my wife came home from a local department store many years ago and shared a horrible customer service experience, something about returning a pair of jeans that fell apart in a few weeks and, after trying to return them, being personally and insensitively challenged by the customer service person and doing it somewhat publicly as well. My wife, offended, left furious. The best part was that my mom was there to hear the story. Okay. The end.

Nope. We found out from my mom that she paid a visit to the store the following day and had a high D conversation with the manager on my wife's behalf. My mom, barely four-foot-seven, never backed down, especially when it came to family. She was fiercely loyal.

And that's the word, *loyal*. My mom was loyal. We should be loyal. Loyalty goes a long way.

Are you always loyal? Because anything but always is not loyal.

ARE YOU BUILDING A CATHEDRAL?

Don't cry because it's over, smile because it happened.
—DR. SEUSS

SOME TIME AGO, I was leading a book study on *The Slight Edge*. A good friend and thought-provoking participant commented on people in the workplace who are not fully engaged. They are there, warming a chair but not really pouring themselves into their role and purpose.

It reminds me of the "The Story of Knowledge: Writing Stories that Guide Organizations into the Future" by Girard J.P. and Lambert S.

> *A man came across three Masons who were working at chipping chunks of granite from large blocks. The first seemed unhappy at his job, chipping away and frequently looking at his watch. When the man asked what it was that he was doing, the first Mason responded, rather curtly, "I'm hammering this silly rock, and I can't wait 'til five when I can go home."*

A second Mason, seemingly more interested in his work, was hammering diligently and when asked what it was that he was doing, answered, "Well, I'm molding this block of rock so that it can be used with others to construct a wall. It's not bad work, but I'll sure be glad when it's done."

A third Mason was hammering at his block fervently, taking time to stand back and admire his work. He chipped off small pieces until he was satisfied that it was the best he could do. When he was questioned about his work, he stopped, gazed skyward, and proudly proclaimed, "I ... am building a cathedral!"

Three men, three different attitudes, all doing the same job.

According to Gallup surveys on employee engagement, less than 30 percent of workers are actually engaged in the workplace. That means three out of ten show up with purpose, focus, and some level of passion for their work. Yet seven out of ten don't! What does that cost companies today!?? In dollars and overall workplace happiness, it has to be devastating.

But then, let's take it a step further: what about the individual? Are we truly engaged in who we are, how we are blessed, and what we love? Not consistently. I think this is a part of the high increase in anxiety and depression we hear about so much today. Not that real physical and psychological issues don't exist, but so many of us just aren't engaged with our own lives. And that is even more devastating.

What drives you? What gives you joy? Is it the things you experience? One speaker said that happiness comes from the word *happenstance*, which is a moment in time and often by chance. We experience it, and it's gone. Happiness is fleeting. How about the gaps in between? That's the difference maker, love the in-between. It's a way of thinking, a philosophy of life. It's an attitude, like the third Mason who was building a cathedral. He wasn't waiting for it to be finished to be happy. He already was, in that moment and the next, knowing why he was doing what he was doing.

ARE YOU DEPENDABLE *REALLY*?

There's no cramming in a test of character,
it always comes as a pop quiz.
—ANDY STANELY

"REALLY" IS THE best part of this title. We met with a handyman for some remodeling work in our master bathroom. A trusted and quite dependable friend referred him to us. We reached out to our would-be handyman and made an appointment. He showed up on time, and we spent forty-five minutes looking at our bathroom, sharing ideas back and forth, and he left with measurements. We really liked this guy and decided to stick with him. He said he'd be back to us in a couple of weeks.

Nothing. I texted. He responded pretty quickly about a family emergency, but no specifics. I responded immediately with my condolences.

Then nothing for two weeks. I texted, "Can you have it to us by this weekend?"

He said, "Yes, I will."

Nothing. I sent another text a few days into the next week asking, "Where are you with this?"

Nothing. I don't know what's going on in his life. But I struggle with not being able to send a ten-second text. Update me. Tell me you don't want the project after all. Just say *something*. It was onto the next handyman for us.

Fourteen years ago, I called three contractors for stump removal and left a message with each of them. One called back the same day; one called a week later. I'm still waiting on the third one. We did business with the first one, and it was done before the second one even called. We needed more work the following year. We made one call.

I believe one of the biggest difference-makers in relationships—family, business, and life—is dependability, which comes from integrity. Do we *always* do what we commit to do? Do we *always* call people back when we say we will? Do we *always* show up as committed? Because sometimes is definitely not dependable.

I think the biggest and yet, least noticed, lack of dependability is in communication. It's the small stuff, one day late, not calling back on time, not delivering on time, and, the coup de grâce, having to be reminded.

Twenty-five years ago, I made a decision with 100 percent integrity. If you need something from me but have to leave a message (email, voicemail, or text), you can immediately cross me off your list. It's as good as done. I know it. You know it.

Let's commit to returning emails on time, returning voicemails on time, meeting all deadlines, and following through on all commitments as expected. And if it's getting tight, reach out and notify people in advance. You'll build so much trust and equity with others.

Be dependable, whatever it takes.

CHAPTER

BE THE LEADER

When there is hope in the future,
there is power in the present.
—ZIG ZIGLAR

IN A RECENT conversation with a client/friend, we were talking about leadership during a crisis, as evidenced by the current state of our country during the COVID crisis.

Leaders need to stand up and demonstrate a perspective of stability and realistic optimism because that is what people need at a time like this, especially amidst the storm of constantly evolving and questionably inconsistent information about current issues and future projections.

I'm not a big fan of flying, partly because it's still a bit disconcerting to me, despite all logic about the safety of flying. Whenever I've flown in the past and experienced heavy turbulence on a flight, the first people I would look toward were the flight attendants. Why did I look to them? I figured that if they weren't scared, why should I be? They know a lot more than I do, and they've been through a lot more than I have. They should know, and I should take my cue from them.

And that's the key during this challenging and uncertain crisis. We need to be the leaders others are looking to, showing that stability and hope. Otherwise, what else are people looking at, social media, twenty-four-hour news, rumors, or hearsay? Who knows what's really accurate and true? But leaders demonstrate confidence, courage, stability, and strength in a crisis. We need more people like that. We need to be those people. Our teams need it. Our families need it. Our community needs it.

According to a Gallup Poll referenced in *Strengths-Based Leadership*, ten thousand followers chose the top-four qualities that drive them to follow specific leaders. They are trust, compassion, stability, and hope.

Let's give people a sense of trust, compassion, stability, and hope in these days. We'll come out stronger for it.

11

BREAKING THROUGH THE CLOUDS

GRIT is Guts, Resilience, Industriousness and
Tenacity. GRIT is the ability to focus, stay determined,
stay optimistic in the face of a challenge, and
simply work harder than the next guy or gal.
—LINDA KAPLAN THALER

I AM NOT a real big fan of flying. I know it's safe, but I still have a bit of uneasiness when I fly, especially when the air is rough, the plane gets tossed around, and the pilot is silent.

Years ago, I was on a flight heading out of Chicago. The weather was pretty bad. It was summer, and there were some very nasty storms all through the area with heavy rain, thunder and lightning, and high winds, all of the stuff that makes for a fantastic and thrilling storm but not for good flying.

We were on the tarmac, and the pilot found an opportunity to get us airborne. As we were about to take off, he announced very directly that this would be a very turbulent ascension, that we were to stay in our seats and keep our seatbelts on. He also told the flight crew to do the same. That killed my idea of watching the crew to see if they were nervous. They were. Yikes. And then we took off.

You know how it works. There's the initial thrust of speed and then the continued acceleration until the plane just has to fly. It seemed like it was an eternity before the nose lifted, and then we were quickly in the air, feeling like we were going straight up. We couldn't see anything through the black and grey clouds. The rain was pouring all around us as we bounced, swayed, dropped, and pushed through the clouds. Logically, I knew we were good. But emotionally, I was anxious and even a little scared, especially with no one talking.

And then, after what seemed like an eternity, we broke through the clouds and were blessed immediately by sunny skies and smooth, clean air. Everything settled down. We leveled off, and eventually the pilot allowed us to move about the cabin. And that's life. Just above or outside the storm we are in, there are sunny skies. There is smooth air. And there is beauty everywhere.

We're all probably dealing with some pretty heavy, daunting, and ambiguous stuff. We have to learn to accept and then push through these challenging times. Challenges push us mentally and physically.

As long as we keep moving forward, or as Dory said in *Finding Nemo*, "Just keep swimming," we'll see those sunny, blue skies once again.

12

CALM UNDER PRESSURE

The Pool of Shared Meaning is the birthplace of synergy.
—FROM CRUCIAL CONVERSATIONS

"PLEASE OPEN THE *door!*" I said with calm but incredibly focused determination.

And she did immediately. Thank God!

What happened? I was standing outside the door of my friend's car with my hand in a precarious spot. It seemed okay while we were talking until she shut the door. The pain was excruciating. Yep, several fingers were trapped in the doorjamb. If you would have asked me what I'd do in this circumstance, I'd tell you there would be an immediate set of words that I cannot type in this article.

And if I had said that, how would she have responded? She would have come unglued, and I'd probably scream more of the same words. She'd become more unglued, and well, you get what I'm saying. My fingers would still be in the door. Not good.

But I didn't. I said calmly and very determined, *"Please open the door."* And she immediately opened it. Only then did I tell her what happened.

Interviewing former Navy Seal Commander Jocko Willink, Tim Ferriss asked him how he handled the extreme nature of combat situations. Jocko offered his classic silent pause and then succinctly answered that he would mentally remove himself and calmly assess the situation to determine the best course of action. This would happen almost instantaneously and would be impossible if he hadn't developed the skill of managing calm under pressure.

You see, this guy was uniquely, physically equipped. He was skilled for battle and had mentally prepared thousands of times over countless scenarios but still needed to be able to think clearly in the heat of the moment. Heart rate explodes, blood and oxygen direct to the muscles for fight or flight, and adrenaline spikes. And the brain is starved, unless your Jocko or someone who's learned to remain calm under pressure.

Reflecting back years later, I was pretty pleased with my reaction. I was calm under pressure.

Next time you have a stressful situation, for example, something goes wrong, a person is rude, the tire blows out, or, like us recently, your pipe bursts. Do you remain calm under pressure?

I recommend it.

13

CATCHING COCKROACHES

*Between stimulus and response there is a space. In
that space is our power to choose our response. In
our response lies our growth and our freedom.*
—VIKTOR E. FRANKL

COLLEGE IS GOOD times, especially the living conditions off campus. Sophomore year found me in a house with ten guys, five in the attic. I thought it was kind of cool. Mom hated it. Senior year had more promise. So we thought.

Late one night, I was deeply sleeping when I must have felt a very slight movement on my neck, the jugular to be exact. Still sleeping, I reached up in reaction, and the itch wiggled in my hand. Bam! I was awake. In a flash, I gripped and flung what I knew was a cockroach all the way across the room. Heebee jeebies! My skin was crawling!

And then it hit me. I threw the cockroach across my room, but it was still in my room. Not good. Go to sleep and hope? No way. I tore the room apart looking for him. I found it just as it slipped into the floor grate. It probably crawled into the darkness and safety of the grate, turned around, and smiled, waiting for me to go back to sleep, which I did. I made sure all the blankets were nowhere near touching the floor and prayed the roach couldn't climb up the bedposts. They can, but thankfully not that night. Or maybe I just didn't notice. Eek!

The bigger problem was not the cockroach. Really the problem was my reaction. It was pure panic and instinct, with no real thinking. Gross as it sounds, I could have thought it through a little more. Maybe grab it and throw it in the toilet or outside. This surely requires a little sacrifice since it would have to be carried to the destination. Or maybe just crush the little bug, even grosser. But I just reacted and paid an additional price.

What are we reacting to? No real thought involved, just reaction. In Stephen Covey's 7 *Habits*, Habit One challenges us to add a choice between stimulus and response. Choice allows for thinking, choosing, and empowering our next step.

The next time something shakes us, stop, think, and then choose the proper response. Reacting requires no thought, usually yielding poor results. Argue lately? It's almost all reacting. Responding empowers us first and usually ends much better. If you add consistency to response, you'll get habits, good ones.

By the way, the cockroach visited me a few days later. I was sitting on the coach, studying something I don't remember. I glanced down, and there he was on the arm, just out for an evening walk. I didn't panic. I chose to get rid of him for good.

14

CHEWY, DOGS, AND FLOWERS

*Biggest question: Isn't it really 'customer helping'
rather than customer service? And wouldn't you
deliver better service if you thought of it that way?*
—JEFFREY GITOMER

AS A CHEWY customer, my wife was recently reading an online article that we found very interesting. A customer had ordered several bags of dog food for their dog. Unfortunately, their dog had passed away prior to the delivery, and when the food arrived, this very sad dog owner reached out to Chewy to ask if he could return the order.

The company advisor quickly replied, "We're so very sorry to hear about your dog passing away. Please keep the dog food and give it away to someone. And we'll remove the charge from your account." Then a few days later, the customer received a sympathy card and flowers from Chewy.

That's customer service! I suspect there is no policy here that made this happen other than allowing and even empowering their customer service people to do whatever it takes and even going ABCD (Above and Beyond the Call of Duty) to effectively serve and wow their customers.

What did Chewy have to lose? A couple of bucks. What did they have to gain? Well, other than supporting and cheering up their customer, there was the viral impact of their good works, which led to my wife seeing and reading the article and me now sharing it with you!

What are some kind and caring actions we can take toward others? Our son, rather than giving a few dollars to a homeless guy on the corner, actually took him to lunch. He gave him a free meal and a listening ear, something he probably hadn't had in a long time. I remember a time we delivered pizza to a homeless man. Maybe he would have liked the cash, but you wouldn't have thought that when we handed him that hot, steaming pizza!

Be grateful and kind to others. You may never know the depth of their situation and the impact of your actions.

C
H
A
P
T
E
R

COFFEE AND SEWERS

Courage doesn't always roar. Sometimes courage is the little
voice at the end of the day that says I'll try again tomorrow.
—MARY ANNE RADMACHER

I LOVE COFFEE very much. I didn't know this as a kid but learned it out of necessity from one of my summer jobs. I worked for a company that cleaned sewer lines. You sometimes see them along a rural road or in town, with trucks on both ends of two manholes leading to the sewer line. They're usually cleaning the line, and I was fortunate to be a part of that!

Our contract was in Manheim, and we operated out of Carlisle. That meant an hourlong drive every morning. On one trip, my partner that day stopped at a convenience store for coffee, came back to the van, left his coffee, and went back in for something else. I was tired. He wasn't there. His coffee was. So I indulged. I didn't really like it, but I began forcing myself to chug a cool cup every morning thereafter. Eventually, I acquired the taste, and I've been hooked ever since.

Back to the sewer cleaning. There's a point to this. Besides cleaning sewer lines, we also patched manholes in residential areas, neighborhoods. One day, we were in a residential development setting up to patch some manholes. Protocol says to wear a raincoat upon entering the manhole and to plug all incoming lines. I remembered one part of the protocol, the raincoat. Much to my dismay, I forgot to plug the lines, and one decided to become very active. It creates a good picture, doesn't it?

There I was patching up a spot when I heard a disparaging sound, immediately understanding what it was. And yes, it erupted all over me. Thankfully, I had the raincoat on, but that's hardly reassuring when a local resident is flushing all over me. My buddy was above ground, rolling around and laughing profusely, exciting times.

What difficult jobs have you had? What did you learn? What can you take away? How could you see it differently? Are you in one right now? Can you find the good?

For me, if it weren't for this job, I may not have discovered coffee, and I got a good story!

16

COMPASSION

More smiling, less worrying. More compassion, less
judgment. More blessed, less stressed. More love, less hate.
—ROY T. BENNETT

I WAS IN my office at my desk making client calls. My office was upstairs in the loft, where the printing company stored paper inventory and had some large format equipment. Most of the time, it was just me up there, but occasionally Joe, the digital format guy, would be up there cutting some foamboard for print.

This time, it was me at my desk, Joe at the equipment, and Troy at his ear. Troy was the production manager and a good one. He was quick, tough, decisive, and sometimes difficult to deal with.

I noticed some slightly higher-volume words as I came off a call and made some notes. On the next call, the background conversation became a bit more animated. It was not too much of a surprise as Troy could sometimes be a little prickly, while Joe was easygoing.

But then it got bad. Voices were raised as emotions soared. I tried to act like nothing was going on, "nothing to see here," but it elevated and almost seemed like a fight would break out.

Then it was quiet. Nothing. I pretended not to notice. I looked back kind of peripherally and saw they were sitting side by side on the step. Troy was facing Joe, whose head was down. I couldn't believe what I was seeing. Rather than Joe getting fired, I saw something quite different, compassion.

Everything changed. I could see Troy completely change his demeanor from hard-edged manager to compassionate friend. Just sitting there talking to Joe, I imagine something switched in Troy because Joe's demeanor was not normal. Joe was never aggressive, argumentative, or coercive. Troy must have thought, *Wait, something's wrong.* Stop. Listen.

I never found out what happened that day, but my respect for Troy skyrocketed. He cared. And he was humble enough to show it. I think I learned to dig deeper in my assessment, conscious or not, of people around me. Troy surprised me, and it was a welcome change.

It taught me to see people better, to make generous assumptions first. I wish I did this all the time, but it's better than it was and getting better every day.

That's the goal, to be better every day.

17

CRABS IN A BUCKET

No matter what your current ability is, effort is what
ignites that ability and turns it into accomplishment.
— CAROL DWECK

I REMEMBER AS a kid being at the beach for summer vacations. On occasion, we'd see people "crabbing" off the dock. Maybe you've done or seen this too. They'd drop those metal cages to the bottom of the bay. The cage is empty, but the food is enticing, and the door is open. After a while, they pull the cages, full of crabs.

And I noticed that as a crab would move to escape, others would simply grab them and pull them back down. It seems like you don't need a gate to keep them in. They have each other!

It reminds me of the Eagle's classic hit, "Hotel California," "You can check out any time you like, but you can never leave." The crabs are the "residents" of the Hotel California!

How many of us are in the hotel, surrounded by crabs and trying to get out? Crabs just love to pull us down into their world of gossip, negativity, misery, blame, and excuses. Crabs don't have anything good to say. Crabs complain about the weather: too hot, too humid, too windy, or too rainy. Crabs complain about the food: too hot, not hot enough, slow service, or too expensive. Mostly crabs complain about others.

These crabs live below the line by choosing blame, excuses, and denial. Let's live above the line by choosing ownership, accountability, and responsibility. What's that saying? "If Bob has a problem with everyone, maybe Bob is the problem." Crabs choose to be victims, unconsciously pulling each other back down into the cage. They create more Bobs.

Let's choose to be like the kid who woke up on Christmas morning, only to find a heap of manure under the tree. Yet the kid is not discouraged because he has an extraordinarily optimistic outlook. His parents find him shoveling manure as he exclaims, "With all this manure, there's gotta be a pony in here somewhere!" Not a crab. Not a Bob.

Be the kid, not the crab. And if you don't stay out of the hotel, you might never leave.

18

A WALKING BILLBOARD

Integrity is doing the right thing, even
when no one is watching.
—UNKNOWN AUTHOR

HAVE YOU EVER waited on tables? Dealt with rude customers? Dealt with customers with no patience or empathy? Have you ever been tipped almost to the point of insult or even stiffed? Have you been on the other side? Have you been that customer? What does that speak of you?

Regardless of the circumstances that may have influenced the poor experience, your actions are your billboard. They are on display for people to judge, right or wrong, and to make broad speculation about what they think you represent.

My daughter waits on tables at a local restaurant. And we've heard a few of these stories. One in particular inspired this article. She waited on a large Christian group who were impatient and rude and let's just say a little tight in the tipping department. The restaurant was clearly understaffed due to the late hour, and my daughter was openly distressed, yet the treatment she received was rash and inappropriate, not met with understanding and patience in any way. A lot more can be said about this experience but won't go into this writing.

It just struck us that regardless of Brittany's faith or that of the other staff serving that night, Christianity took a hit, not for its foundation, but for the billboard on display. This billboard, in my opinion, was inaccurate and unfair, but on display just the same. And right or wrong, some will attribute the actions of those people to their understanding of Christianity. "I remember meeting a group of Christians—impatient, rude, and cheap …"

Most who are reading this know where I stand in my faith, which goes for my daughter as well. So please understand that writing this isn't easy, yet that's just the reason to write it.

Everything we do is a walking billboard for what others associate with us: our marriage, our company, our job, our country, and, absolutely, our faith.

What's your billboard saying?

19

DEFENSE IS A LOUSY OFFENSE

Businesses are not dishonest or greedy, people are.
Thus, a business, successful or not, is merely a
reflection of the character of its leadership.
—TRUETT CATHY

MANY OF MY clients know me enough to know that my wife and I love to visit breweries. We even schedule getaways around a good brewery we've heard of. The special craft beer is really good, but the connection, conversation, and fun are the real value in our marriage.

We have one that we really love, and we've been going for a few years. The beer is amazing. The vibe is perfect, and the people are absolutely awesome ... usually.

A few months ago, my wife saw a deal on their website. Yes, she signed up to get notifications. It was for a free $25 gift card with the purchase of a $100 gift card. Well, we'd be going anyway, so this was a no-brainer for us.

This may get tricky to follow, but please stay with me. So we bought the $100 gift card, which included another free $25 gift card, and gave a 15 percent tip. Yeah, that was silly, but they turn that POS on you, and you have to hit "custom" to change it. So I clicked the next best. I always tip, but not typically on a gift card since I'll tip when we use it. Anyway, you do the math.

When we got home and looked at the receipt, we were charged for the $25 free card. We paid $125 plus tip! No big deal. We'd just sort it out when we got there again.

I happened to be driving by one day and decided to get it taken care of. And that's when I met her. As I approached, I tried to figure out how to present this without confusion. So I did my best. She was confused and, I think, a little embarrassed. And then she got angry. No matter how soft my approach—and trust me, I pushed myself because I could see she was uncomfortable and tabling it in frustration, directing it back at me—she didn't understand, defaulted to defensiveness, and asked for no help.

I stood there and was dumbfounded. How could I have approached that differently? I teach this stuff! Looking back, I felt I approached it well. I can get worked up when someone challenges my integrity, but I stayed full-on Cool Hand Luke, you know, Paul Newman. If you don't, look it up. So I waited, frustrated. I love this place and these people. And now this was messing with me. I don't remember the last time I'd been treated that way in a service situation.

Eventually, she came back, and another server, who heard everything and knew my disappointment and frustration, came to help her. They worked it out. She, with a little attitude, fixed it and never apologized.

I know she was confused and embarrassed and clearly handled things poorly. And there may have been some other life situation. But a sincere apology would not have made any of that worse and, in fact, would have made her feel better.

Conflict is challenging. It takes courage and humility. And it's not guaranteed to be productive even if you do it right. It takes two. But here's the lesson. Do it anyway. It improves our odds and makes us better.

20 CHAPTER

DISAGREE AND COMMIT

*Individual commitment to a group effort—
that is what makes a team work, a company
work, a society work, a civilization work.*
—VINCE LOMBARDI

YEARS AGO, WHEN our kids were much younger, my wife and I always strived to build strong family connections. We still do today, but they're just different as everyone is fully grown. Back then, we did much more together as a family, and the kids actually enjoyed it.

One problem we had was getting everyone to agree on what we would do in the evenings. Many nights, we would sit around and debate about what movie to watch, what game to play, which puzzle to build, and so forth. We eventually fell on an idea that turned out to be very effective. We chose a couple of designated family nights, maybe two or three specific days that we decided to do family stuff together in the evenings. With three kids and three different ideas for how to have fun, coming up with a consensus was difficult, if not impossible.

So we decided as a team that we'd assign a night for each family member. While we'd always consider everyone's input, ultimately whoever owned the night made the final decision. Knowing their night was coming gave them a little more willingness to commit to a decision when it wasn't their night to choose. They still might have disagreed, but they had to commit if the plan were to work. "Disagree and commit" was the rule. And it worked most of the time.

When team members have a chance to weigh in on a decision, they typically will be much more likely to buy in on the decision. Why? Because they were heard. And that means their ideas were valued. And it makes it easier for them to still disagree yet fully commit to the team decision.

Patrick Lencioni cites commitment as part of the third element of the 5 Behaviors of a Cohesive Team. Strong teams don't force consensus because that is very difficult to reach. Getting everyone to agree always, have you tried that?

Consensus is nice, but if not, then disagree and commit. It makes for an excellent team.

21

DOG ON A NAIL ... THE
REST OF THE STORY

You can't move people to action unless you first move
them with emotion ... The heart comes before the head.
—JOHN MAXWELL

YOU'VE ALL PROBABLY heard the story written long ago by Les Brown, a well-known motivational speaker.

> A man walks into an old general store. As he moves through the aisles, he notices a dog lying beside the checkout counter where the owner is sitting. The dog is whimpering and whining when he walks in, and again he notices him doing the same thing when he approaches the owner to check out.
>
> He asks the owner, "Your dog seems to be in pain. What's the problem?"
>
> The owner responds, "Oh, that's just old Rover. That's where he lays and naps every day. He's

whimpering and whining because over time a nail has worn through the floorboard, and it hurts him."

"Why doesn't he just move?" says the visitor.

The owner replies, "Well, I guess it just doesn't hurt enough to move."

I've often referenced that silly story when trying to help people understand that they're griping and complaining are worthless if they don't have an interest in the solution. Ever been around them? They know there's a problem, but they keep wallowing in it. Whatever good advice that's offered, it's irrelevant because the victim doesn't want the solution. The solution is never what he's after; it's the audience.

Well, I thought about this the other day when I was lamenting over people who are like the dog. I can't stand when people harp on their issues with absolutely no interest in any solutions. Why? Because that would take away their excuse to complain.

And then I realized that I was complaining about these people, which kind of made me part of the problem. My response to their lack of responsibility was frustrating me. I wrote an article years ago, "Is It Better to Engage the Fool or to Be the Fool?" If the dog on the nail continues to bother me, I guess I am also the Fool.

So the next time I see or hear a dog on a nail, the Fool, I'll just smile and walk on by.

22 CHAPTER

GET IN THE WAY

Formal education will make you a living; self-education will make you a fortune.
—JIM ROHN

EVERYONE SELLS. SOME of us sell for a living. We sell ideas, products, and services; we sell good feelings and solutions to problems.

But in today's world, the challenge to get people's attention enough to even say "hello" is getting more difficult. People are moving at breakneck speed, and the demands of distraction are everywhere. Social media has allowed tremendous exposure with little depth. And depth is what sells. At least that's where the real selling occurs. Eye contact, relationship, engagement, authenticity, trust, and competency are much better developed in person. And with all the technology we have, people still buy from people.

We need to get back to the old-fashioned key to sales. See more people. Get in the way. How do you do that? You find ways to get in the way.

Be the one to meet your prospect at the networking event. Be the one to reach out to your client without being prompted by a project. You call and set a meeting to discuss their yearly goals and challenges. You set the conversation to learn about their growth objectives. You see them about who else you should be talking to. You ask them how you can serve them better. Just go see them. Who? Your customers, your prospects, your past customers, your vendors, your connections, and your friends of influence.

Remember to be a P.E.A.K. performer.

- P = Perspective. It's what you *think* about what you do.
- E = Expertise. It's how *well* you do what you do.
- A = Action. It's how *often* you do what you should be doing.
- K = Knowledge. It's how *knowledgeable* you are about what you do.

For you salespeople, it's about just being in front of people who can buy from you or lead you to those who can: touch base meetings, review meetings, opportunity meetings, lunch meetings, breakfast meetings, networking events, business events, speaking events, and strategic meetings. What else? Do what it takes to just get in front of more of the right people.

If you did not hit your sales goals last year, I'd bet you just didn't see enough people. Set some goals this year and be the guy everyone knows, likes, and trusts. You'll be glad you did.

23

GET OFF YOUR AGENDA

One of the greatest gifts you can give is the gift of attention.
—JIM ROHN

PEOPLE MATTER. YEARS ago, if you would have asked me if I were a people- or task-oriented person (understanding it's not mutually exclusive), I would have said people. Now I'm not so sure.

About fifteen years ago, our neighbor across the street bought a new shed. We didn't have a shed, if you can believe that. So we asked if we could have their old shed. And not really having a great way to dispose of it, he gladly complied.

Now to get it to our house. Maybe 150 yards from the current spot through his side yard, the street, our side yard, and down in the backyard corner. Easy, right?

The problem was transportation. So with the help of a friend who was a construction-type guy—finish carpenter, to be exact—we were off and running. Given his background, I trusted his way was the best way. We began with manpower, a truck, and some PVC pipes. That's right. PVC pipes were the key mode of transportation. We had no way to lift it onto a truck and no truck big enough anyway. To add to the challenge, the shed had no solid base, so the side wood slats would have to roll on the pipes. That got messy. It was extremely slow and unsteady. An hour in, we hadn't gotten very far.

Then my neighbor a few houses away saw us while he was cutting his grass. He stopped and yelled, "Do you need any help!"

I said, "Sure."

He grabbed a digging iron and headed down.

Six hours later, we got the shed where we wanted it, and he turned back to his lawn. A lot happened in between, but goal accomplished.

The key to this story was my neighbor who, on a whim, offered some help. I'm pretty sure he didn't think to himself, *Hmmm, I'd like to take a six-hour detour from my personal agenda—cutting my grass—and drive myself out of my mind helping my neighbor roll a shed on PVC pipes to his yard.* But he did. He got off his agenda and stepped into ours.

Looking back, I am very impressed. Who does that? Well, I need to do that more. While tasks are important, people are so much more important. And I'm working on that every day. How about you? Do you need to occasionally get off your agenda?

By the way, I still have my neighbor's digging iron.

24

HALF-AND-HALF

*You cannot enjoy others until you enjoy yourself because
you cannot give to others what you do not have.*
—John C. Maxwell

THE OTHER DAY, I was looking for the half-and-half for my coffee. I had just finished one the day before and knew we had picked some up on our recent grocery run.

But I couldn't find it. You know how it works. You first look where it usually is, and then you look in that alternative location. And if you don't see it, you begin looking through the shelves. I did all of this, found nothing, and closed the fridge, thinking, *I know we bought some.* So then I checked the garage fridge, even though I knew it wouldn't be there. And lo and behold, it wasn't. Okay, where is this stuff?!

I decided to re-engage my search in the main fridge, with the same process. The likely place? No. The alternative place? No. Okay, go shelf by shelf, top to bottom. At the bottom, I pulled out the half-and-half and looked around, only to finally notice I was holding what I was looking for! What?!

You probably know what happened. It was a half-quart bottle, which we never buy. We always buy the smaller pint-sized one. I knew I was looking for half-and-half, but my brain pulled up the pint-sized image, and that was the extent of my search results. Find the pint-sized carton, and you'll find the half-and-half. That's what my brain told me.

Have you been there? It's amazing how I didn't see it. This speaks so much to our narratives. We see what we choose to see, without consciously vetting things through. We just go to what we think we know.

We probably all need to be more self-aware and socially aware. These false narratives may be the cause of many relationship challenges at home and work.

I wonder what narratives are driving most of my thoughts and how can I start fresh, with no narrative, just information, moving forward? How about you? That reminds me of the cliché, "A mind is like a parachute; if it isn't open, it doesn't work."

While we often toss clichés aside, perhaps this one needs a bit more attention.

25

HAWAII FIVE-0

*A leader is one who knows the way, goes
the way, and shows the way.*
—JOHN MAXWELL

HAVE YOU EVER driven a pontoon boat? My first experience
was one to remember. Probably twenty years ago, my wife and I were
on a trip with two other couples down in Marco Island, Florida. One
of the days, we decided to rent a pontoon boat to take out into some
of the tributaries inside the shoreline. I was the leader, the driver of
the boat. None of us had any experience. So out we went with me at
the helm.

A couple of interesting things happened while I was the captain,
the self-appointed leader. First, while pulling a tube carrying my
highly organized, detailed, and intelligent civil engineer friend, I
turned into the rope, and he was promptly cut off. The rope was cut
completely in half. I was somewhat redeemed when, while we pulled
in the rope, we noticed several knotted areas along the way. We just
added one more.

Later, again pulling another engineer friend, this one structural engineering, I ran the boat aground. We all got out and pulled the boat free. And once again, I resumed my esteemed role at the helm.

A little later, we were trolling along the deeper and wider part of the tributary. We pulled close to a large yacht. It was moving a little too slowly for my patience, so I tried to pass it. Big mistake. The huge wake from the yacht, combined with my aggressive driving, led me to my best and last blunder.

My seven-month-pregnant wife was in the very front of the pontoon. I was trying to pass this lazy yacht and gunned it just as we hit the top of a large wake. We speared to the bottom and, consequently, drove a huge wave to roll directly over the front of our boat. Can anyone say "Hawaii Five-O"? I thought for sure everything on the front deck would be flushed into the water, including my wife. Thankfully, she just got soaked!

Despite my small success there, I was promptly fired.

What was the lesson my passengers learned that day? Be careful who is leading you.

26

INTO THE FIRE

Do the thing we fear, and death of fear is certain.
—RALPH WALDO EMERSON

I WAS PROBABLY twenty years old, between my junior and senior years as a marketing major at Shippensburg University. My mom had a connection with an old friend who recently started an employment service, offering services of employee placement for full- and part-time work to clients. Since I was in marketing and this person needed a salesperson, the deal was set. I would be that salesperson.

I showed up in May to pursue this sales job until my senior year began again in August. Keep in mind I had zero direct sales experience and my marketing major offered no classes in sales. There was a class called sales management, but no sales. Imagine that.

As I went into the office, she directed me to the back of the room, to her office. Just inside the door, to the right, was a small desk with a chair, phone, and fishbowl. The fishbowl was the result of the latest Chamber of Commerce Business Show, and it was full of business cards. She directed me to the desk and said to begin calling the names on the cards in the fishbowl. Um, what? She sat down at her desk, same office, just a few feet away.

"You mean just call these names and sell with you right here?" That's what I was thinking.

I was terrified. And I have no memory after that. I must have made some calls because I was invited back the next day and eventually graduated to cold calls in the field. What a blessing!

Since that first official sales experience, I've faced many other scary, challenging, and stomach-churning situations over the years. But nothing was quite like that. And yet I overcame. Just like you do.

The greatest fear was before making the calls and in between the calls, not the actual calls. Why? Because before and in between, I was thinking. During the calls, I was doing.

And that's the key, and the title to a great book about it, *Feel the Fear and Do It Anyway*. The more we choose to just get into action, the less we'll fear. In fact, in another great book by Dr. David Schwartz, my main takeaway was this statement, "Action cures fear." So good.

What do you fear? What is holding you back? What do you need to do but don't want to do? The great Dale Carnegie told us exactly what to do, "If you want to conquer fear, don't sit at home and think about it. Go out and get busy."

27

INVISIBLE

Research indicates that employees have three prime needs:
Interesting work, recognition for doing a good job, and
being let in on things that are going on in the company.
—ZIG ZIGLAR

THERE IS A scene in the movie *What Women Want* starring Mel Gibson and Helen Hunt about an employee (played by Judy Greer) struggling with thoughts of suicide because she feels like nobody even notices her ever. After Mel experiences something that enables him to know what women around him are thinking, he becomes aware of this coworker's thoughts, and he's able to do something about it.

Fortunately, we cannot hear others' thoughts—thoughts of insecurity, unfulfillment, and failure—but that's not a good excuse for not being aware that people need to be recognized, edified, and supported. You've likely heard the reference that respect is like air. The moment you don't have it, it becomes the most important thing you need.

Something else works quite the same way, recognition. But unlike air, its nonexistence is virtually unnoticeable day to day, invisible. Since we all pretty much live day to day, we think we are okay without a lot of recognition. And if we don't think we need it, we project that on others, meaning they don't need it either.

According to Gallup Research, less than 30 percent of American employees are engaged at the workplace, and worldwide, it's less than 13 percent. Let me tell you about people—our teams and our coworkers and maybe our families. More people than we realize feel unnoticed, unnecessary, and irrelevant. That does not make for a highly engaged person at work or home. And it's usually our fault. We don't slow down and do these seemingly little things that we ultimately know makes a huge difference.

Do your people feel relevant? Do your people feel they're needed? Do they even feel like you see them? You have much more influence than you think. What you think means more than you think.

Forget all the big, creative, time-consuming ways to recognize. Well, do those if you're willing, but don't let them and the time it takes to do them stand in the way. Just say "thank you." Just use people's names. Just ask how their weekend was and pause for the answer.

Just notice people. Just tell them they matter. Just tell them they're needed and appreciated. Do it authentically. Mean it. And keep it consistent. Lack of consistency kills trust.

And remember, a culture, *your culture*, is a consistent set of actions.

28

IT'S ABOUT THE REPS

*Every action you take is a vote for the type of
person you'd like to become. No single instance
will transform your beliefs, but as the votes build
up, so does the evidence of your new identity.*
—JAMES CLEAR

YEARS AGO, I read a story about a professor teaching a class in
pottery. He instructed the students to break out into two groups. One
group's assignment was to create as many pottery bowls as possible
in one session. Their focus was quantity, and they would be graded
based on the total weight of what they produced. The second group
was to create just one bowl in the session. And they would be graded
on the quality of that bowl.

When the session was over, each group presented their pottery bowls.
After the grades were distributed, the teacher asked the first group to
display all the bowls they created and the second group to display their
one bowl. He'd made a mark on the bottom of the quality bowl so that
nobody could clearly differentiate it from all the bowls.

Then he asked the entire class to determine the bowl with the highest level of quality. What they picked was a surprise. It was one of the bowls from the group focused on quantity, not the one focused on quality. The lesson: Quantity leads to quality by force of repetition and the natural progression of progress. That's it. It's all about the reps.

As we come into the new year and cross the threshold into 2021, most people have one obvious goal, end COVID.

But now ask what proactive things you can do to impact the most important parts of your life in 2021. I mean real change, if that's worthwhile. Family, health, faith, income, finances, hobbies, education, and career, what matters most? Then what can you do daily to grow in those areas? It's actually pretty simple.

And then apply the quantity principle. Don't try to make it great right away. Just make it a little bit better every day.

Do reps often. Do them consistently. And then keep doing it.

29

JUST GIVE IN

*We don't drift in good directions. We discipline
and prioritize ourselves there.*
—ANDY STANLEY

THAT'S IT! I'M doing it this time. Tomorrow morning, I'm getting up and going to the gym. I am. Seriously!

The next morning, the alarm clock buzzes at 5:00 a.m. Are you kidding me?! I'm snoozing. I'll get up in a bit, right? The result was no gym.

Part of the problem is that we made the decision while we were wide awake! When we had to execute the decision, we were barely awake. And often the body supersedes the mind. No gym. People give up what they want most in life, good health and vitality, for what they want right now, comfort.

My friend used to say to me, "Mike, you can make money, or you can make excuses, but you can't have both." You can substitute anything you might want for money, like good health, good relationships, or a good marriage.

The other day, it occurred to me that it really comes down to just giving in. We can continue with the constant regret of poor decisions or finally just give in to the self-discipline of execution. It's the age-old Nike tagline, "Just Do It!"

Self-discipline sounds so regimented, controlling, and downright miserable. It took a long time for me to see that self-discipline looks and feels a lot better on the back end than it does up front. But if we'll just give in and do what we say we should do, based on where we want to be and who we want to be, we'll eventually be on the other side of self-discipline. Freedom, my friends, is anything but controlling or miserable.

Andy Stanley hosts a terrific podcast called *Your Next Move*. And the tagline of this podcast is the essence of this message, "Better decisions, fewer regrets."

Let's give in and make the decisions to fulfill the life and experiences we want. No regrets.

30

LITTLE BEETLES OF WORRY

ACTION IS WORRY'S worst enemy.

I read this story in Dale Carnegie's fabulous book, *How to Stop Worry and Start Living.*

> On the slope of Long's Peak in Colorado lies the ruin of a gigantic tree. Naturalists tell us that it stood for some four hundred years. It was a seedling when Columbus landed at San Salvador, and half grown when the Pilgrims settled at Plymouth. During the course of its long life, it was struck by lightning fourteen times, and the innumerable avalanches and storms of four centuries thundered past it. It survived them all. In the end, however, an army of beetles attacked the tree and leveled it to the ground. The insects ate their way through the bark and gradually destroyed the inner strength of the tree by their tiny but incessant attacks. A forest giant which age had not withered, nor lightning blasted, nor storms subdued, fell at last before beetles so small that a man could crush them between his forefinger and his thumb.

Isn't it so true?!

Do you worry? Are you anxious? Is much of life a pre-play of negative outcomes? If you could download and categorize your thoughts, what percentage would be a form of worry? Yikes!

Worry is a negative use of imagination. And the beetles are the classic metaphor for worry in our lives. It eats away at our joy, our fulfillment, our attitude, and our progress. It invites negative narratives and so often sets the course of our days, weeks, and years.

If we need help, we should get help. Otherwise, let's take control. Let's be conscious of the little beetles and how to defeat them.

It's said that the enemy of success is not negativity. That's too obvious; it's mediocrity. Now that's sneaky. Just like a beetle.

CHAPTER

LOYALTY ALASKAN STYLE

Indifference and neglect often do much
more damage than outright dislike.
—J. K. ROWLING

OUR DAUGHTER, MADI, loves anything scary, terrifying, and potentially dangerous, to a point. Recently, my wife and I, along with Madi and her boyfriend, were reminiscing about scary things that have happened to us. Madi asked my wife to re-share one such situation.

I was away at a rare evening business meeting, and my wife and the kids were going through the bedtime routine at our house. This was when the kids were little and they still appreciated these things. They're twenty, twenty-five, and twenty-eight (and married) and don't seem to want to be tucked in anymore. Oh well, next generation up!

Anyway, I was supposed to be home soon. While reading to the kids, they all heard a noise downstairs, clearly sounding like the kitchen door opening, the one I would typically use. After a pause and expecting to hear me coming up the steps, the silence made my wife curious. She called for me from the top of the stairs and waited. No response.

She called again, not really concerned because they were convinced they heard me come in. No response. She kind of decided it was nothing and went back to the kids. Then they all heard what they thought were pots and pans, things moving in the kitchen as if I were there.

Amy went to the stairs and called again. Nothing. This was now officially scary! She didn't know what to do other than send the kids to their rooms with doors closed. She was so scared, so she called her twin sister in Alaska. They're very close, and that's all she could think to do.

Beth listened and then promptly apologized and said, "I have to go. I'll call you back."

Amy couldn't believe her sister would end the call when she clearly needed her, but she waited. Shortly after, the police showed up. They checked the entire house, inside and out, and found nothing. They completely understood Amy's fear and validated the need for the police. Then the officer finished by saying, "Calling us was the right thing to do, but we'll get here faster if the call doesn't come from Alaska!"

We never identified what they heard that night. But we do know one thing. Beth doesn't mess around when it comes to her sister and family! Loyalty rules the relationship.

Loyalty is one of the characteristics my longtime friend and mentor constantly touted. I understand why.

MENTAL AUDIT

*Our thought are traders that make lose the good
we might oft win, by fearing to attempt.*
—SHAKESPEARE

HAVE YOU EVER done a financial audit, tracking every penny spent over thirty days? Revealing, isn't it? The picture we have is always in the moment: buy a cup of coffee, grab a pizza or quick bite, meet a client over lunch, make a quick stop at the convenience store, see a movie, have drinks out, and so forth. Alone, they seem safe, reasonable. Maybe.

Enter, the Latte Principle. A couple tracked the lattes they both bought to and from Starbucks every weekday. Five bucks times two people times two stops times five days times fifty-two weeks equals $5,200 per year! And how much do you have to earn to keep $5,200?! It's worth it in the smallness of the moment, but is it when seen in this new light? For some, the answer is a resounding yes. For most, it's not.

Some of us have taken this audit plan, how we spend our time, to the next level. Have you tried it? Track all actions 24/7 in fifteen-minute blocks. Yuck! I've tried. I got a few days in but lost my edge.

It takes tremendous awareness, organization, and grit to pull this off correctly. Even a soft audit, listing what you do but not chronologically, just a list, can help. That does work and has helped me dump some sneaky time stealers while gaining more conscious control over other high-priority actions.

Have you ever heard the phrase, "We become what we think about"? So let's go there, the coup de grâce, the Big Cheese, the Grand Poobah, your thinking. What if you could do a thought audit over thirty days? How many thoughts do you have in a day?

Imagine an app that tuned into your brain and tracked and categorized all of your thoughts, even ranking them in frequency. Scary!

And yet this might be the one scientific discovery that could change everything. Self-awareness would soar. We would actually know so much about ourselves, how many negative, useless, self-deprecating, fearful, anxiety-ridden, and destructive thoughts we actually have and how much these are about the one in the mirror.

Oh, that's why I feel this way. That's why I struggle with this person or that new opportunity. That's why I am where I am.

Here's where we get into real self-awareness. We may not have a way to track every thought, but neuroscience has discovered how to track the pathways and how they get there. Consistent thoughts repeat. Repetition creates ruts, which turn into the neuropathways we unintentionally or intentionally choose. Those pathways or ruts pull us in line with that thinking, without thinking about it, a habit.

Getting control of our thoughts is possible. The how of this is much more complicated than I can explain or truly understand. But the science is out there.

The problem isn't that we don't have the app to tell us our thoughts. We already know. Remember, we become what we think about. So let's just get better about what we think about. How? Your inputs infect or protect. Choose what you want and find the resources that drive that thinking.

Find the books, the people, and any resources to influence the right thinking, and eventually, you'll slowly change your thinking.

You'll still become what you think about. And that's a good thing.

33

MIND OVER MATTER

*If you believe it will work out, you will see
opportunities; if not, you will see obstacles.*
—WAYNE DYER

A FEW DAYS ago, I picked up my annual cold for the season. It didn't last long, a little in the throat and then two days of runny nose, sneezing, and a leaking eye. Yes, just one eye. Strangely, only the right side of my face was leaking, which is not unusual for me but definitely weird.

Anyway, my typical cold includes a lot of leaking from the designated side, of course, sneezing, and blowing. It's not a big deal, but it is a bit uncomfortable, especially when I'm around other people. Plus the COVID thing. After one sneeze, everyone runs!

On Saturday, during the height of this experience, I went to the climbing gym with my son. I leaked the whole way there. I even threw some tissues in my shorts expecting more drainage while climbing. But the next time anything leaked was on my way home.

Let the flow return! But why was it silent for ninety minutes? I didn't take any medicine, and that rarely works anyway, unless it's NyQuil, which basically makes the real me nonexistent for forty-eight hours. Is there anything worse? No, thank you.

Mind over matter really does work. It just takes a shifted focus or distraction. What we focus on gets bigger, and everything else gets smaller. I focused on climbing, learning from Mitch, and sending my project, which I did. And I forgot about the cold.

I think most of us know that distraction changes our focus and can actually mask any discomfort, pain, or even anxiety we have. You don't feel it if you don't think about it.

Distraction is easy, but it proves you can control your mind with the right focus. The challenge is how to focus on what we want, not what we have if what we have is not what we want. Read that one again!

Barney from *How I Met Your Mother* said it best, "When I'm sick, I stop being sick and be awesome instead."

The only way out is by being proactive. Choose what to think about by taking action or, a little more difficult, purposeful thought through positive imagination, meditation, reflection, and prayer.

What are you thinking about that you want to stop thinking about? What negative thoughts are festering in your mind that you need to replace with positive, motivating, and inspiring thoughts?

34

NO PERIPHERALS

Sow a thought, reap an action; sow an action,
reap a habit; sow a habit, reap a character;
sow a character, reap a destiny.
—STEPHEN COVEY

A LONG, LONG time ago, I stopped to ask for directions at a Rite Aid parking lot. Yes, this is before GPS. I just lost most of you.

It wasn't hard to find someone there. In this strange time, people talked to others in public! And this guy was good. He shared the directions to a T, and I was off. I got lost immediately and had to do it all over again.

What went wrong? I didn't have peripherals. Peripherals are the sidelines. We don't see the sidelines because we haven't been there.

The first guy had them, and I didn't. Think about a time you gave someone instructions, directions to do something? Probably today.

Peripherals are the things you see in your mind based on previous experience. When giving instruction, you see the sidelines because you've been there. The other guy doesn't. He sees only what you say, no peripherals.

He sees the barn by the left turn and the farmland on the right. He sees the gas station and CVS after the third turn. He sees the destination with all its surroundings. And even if he adds some of those, all it does is complicate things!

We don't have the benefit of Google directions when learning a new task or being instructed to organize an event or complete a complicated project. We might have written instructions, but still no peripherals. Communication will be a lot easier this way.

So the next time you delegate, equip, train, coach, advise, or simply communicate, know they might not have your peripherals. That will create more empathy, understanding, and education so you can communicate clearly, concisely, and effectively.

It'll also inspire the most important communication tool, patience.

35

**C
H
A
P
T
E
R**

OH, THE FREEDOM!

Accountability breeds response-ability.
—STEPHEN COVEY

YEARS AGO, I remember being frustrated in my sales career. It's not that I wasn't working hard or even having success, but I knew I could and should do more. As a sales guy, I had no problem understanding intellectually what I should be doing to grow my book of business. And the top priority was lead generation.

Keep in mind, this was in the early 1990s, and email, texting, and websites, for the most part, didn't exist. So lead generation was primarily old school. Knock on doors. Get a contact. Drop something off, but not everything. And call back to set an appointment.

I didn't like to knock on doors, but I especially didn't like to call back within three days. It was the furthest action from a new sale and yet, to me, the hardest. In sales, we define this as "call reluctance." I did the calls, but not consistently. It was sporadic and painful, and so the pressure was on me 24/7, like carrying anchors.

Then I learned about time blocking and self-discipline and had just been in a workshop about values. I identified one of my top values as personal integrity. Eventually, that became integrity. Between my thoughts around time blocking, self-discipline, and personal integrity, I decided I would always do what I said I'd do, no exceptions. Once the commitment was made, it was done. Why? Because I hated regrets. Not doing what I knew I should be doing.

And I followed through, setting dedicated blocks of time in my calendar for making those calls. I didn't set a quantity goal; I set a time goal. I scheduled a personal appointment to make calls. And as long as I honored that time for its purpose, regardless of results, I had no regrets.

Well, the results were fantastic. But that paled in comparison to what I really learned. By executing this habit, I became much more confident in myself because I did what I said I'd do. I was personally accountable. I didn't carry the burden of calls all week long, just for two designated hours.

The habit of self-discipline led me to an identity of personal integrity, the ultimate success. Identity goes much further than planning and making calls; it's who I am and who you are.

Following through on all your commitments will lead to a remarkable sense of freedom because you don't have to think about it. You just do it. Because that's who you are.

What regrets do you have? These are things you know you should be doing and you know you're not doing. Something is holding you back. Build self-discipline. Do it for a few months. Don't look back. Regardless of outcomes, you'll begin to change your identity by following through.

And our identity drives our beliefs, which drives our behavior, which is what we are all trying to improve in the first place!

36

PAY YOURSELF FIRST

Chains of habit are too light to be felt until
they are too heavy to be broken.
—WARREN BUFFET

YOU THINK YOU know what this article is about, but what you are thinking is only a small part of this big picture.

Yes, one of the first rules of finance is to pay yourself first! Most don't do it. Some never knew it. No one who gets it would deny its truth, especially after years of not doing it. So, yes, pay yourself first. And yet there's so much more.

I was meeting with a good friend recently, and we were discussing habits for personal growth. You know, the normal stuff—faith, family, marriage, health, and so forth. And while he was talking about health habits, he said, "You know, pay yourself first."

I gotta say, I always thought of that concept only in terms of finances, never everything else. But ultimately, when we honor our health by taking care of ourselves every day, our spirituality by investing in faith every day, our marriage and family by learning and applying lessons daily, and our minds by reading daily, all of that is under the same concept of "pay yourself first." Get these things into your schedule first. Take care of yourself first.

That last one seems like a selfish one. Take care of yourself first? What about our family and friends? What about our church community, business, and career relationships? Yes, we take care of them, help them, serve them, and do our best to make a positive, lasting influence in their lives. But how good of a job do we do when we're not right? If we are beaten down, sleep-deprived, low in energy and vitality, and even unhealthy, what kind of impact can we really have?

Think of it this way: You're flying with your kids on an airplane. An emergency occurs, and the oxygen masks come down. What is our natural response? Get the mask on our kids first. Right move? No! We are actually told to do just the opposite, to take care of us first. If we don't get us right, we won't get anyone else right.

So let's take my friend's excellent advice: Pay yourself first.

37

PEEP FROGS

*Human beings always act and feel and perform
in accordance with what they imagine to be true
about themselves and their environment.*
—DR. MAXWELL MALTZ

DURING THIS COVID crisis, I imagine most of us are trying to find ways to be active, find fun, and enjoy time with our families while staying at home. To me, that doesn't have to mean staying inside. I know that some feel that's the safest thing to do. Outside of extenuating circumstances, I respectfully disagree. Outside is almost always the healthiest place to be. With fresh air, sunshine, and space, outside rocks!

Lately, though, outside hasn't really rocked. It's rained, and it's been cold and windy, not a great recipe for being outside.

I was walking around our yard with my wife just the other day. It was a dreary, rainy day, and we were taking advantage of a brief period in between the rain. I must admit I was kind of complaining about the rainy, cold April we've been having, limiting our outside adventures.

I'm also a little sneaky when it comes to negativity, masking it in sarcasm.

But then we noticed the peep frogs in our pond singing gloriously. And it occurred to me: the rain and cold sure didn't bother them. They chirped and peeped just as much in the chilly, rainy forties as they did in the warm and sunny sixties. They just do what they do, despite what they cannot control.

This is a great lesson for me, one I already know, but one I needed to have reinforced in such a unique and interesting manner on this day. I appreciate all those little guys peeping proudly! It's one of my favorite spring sounds! And despite COVID and March-like weather in late April, they keep on peeping.

So that's my plan. Keep on peeping, rain or shine.

38

PLANNING LIKE A PUZZLER

*The essence of Tiny Habits is this: Take a
behavior you want, make it tiny, find where it fits
naturally in your life, and nurture its growth.*
—B. J. FOGG

A FEW WEEKS ago, I saw my wife on the floor with Emmett,
our four-year-old grandson. They were putting a puzzle together. It's
one of those "big piece" puzzles for little guys like him. How adorable?!

Before offering any help, she decided to see what his little four-year-
old mind would do on its own.

He dumped the pieces and picked one up and then another to see if
they matched. Of course, even with so few pieces, finding a match
like that is highly unlikely and, to a four-year-old, very frustrating.
Mercifully, she decided it was time to teach him the right way, or at
least get him started.

She then explained and demonstrated what most of us common
puzzlers would identify as best practices for effective puzzling, which,
as you'll read, works with time management as well.

1. Spread out the pieces so they're flat and easy to pick up. *To complete your project or prioritize your day, you need to clearly see everything in front of you.*

2. Flip all the pieces to the picture side for even more clarity. *With it all laid out, you can see everything. You're no longer up against the "elephant."*

3. Organize all edges according to the consistency of color and images, things that look like they might fit together with the picture. *Your fog is clearing, and decisions are much easier.*

4. With that strategy, build the frame. *Your priorities are in your schedule. What gets scheduled gets done.*

5. Organize the inside pieces according to pictures and designs.

For the five hundred-piece-plus puzzles, us adults often build the pictures separately and outside the frame. My mother-in-law used a spatula to surgically add the outside picture into the frame. It was impressive. I usually try to pick it up and slide it over the edge, often failing in the process.

That's it. You have built the puzzle! *That nagging project is now complete! And it wasn't that hard when you decided to patiently build the puzzle the right way!*

As you can see, it occurred to me that best practices in puzzling are a great lesson in time management. Most time management challenges aren't about not having time. They're more about how you understand your tasks and how to chunk them down into small pieces, organize, schedule them, and then execute. And voilà! The "picture" is complete.

That means first scheduling fifteen to thirty minutes to download the mess in your brain to paper, which is necessary to complete your task or project. Second, schedule steps you've identified into palatable chunks of time in your calendar. All you've done is create space to build the framework. No progress yet, right? Wrong! You're mentally halfway done! Isn't it true that the toughest part of getting on the treadmill is the pondering before, "Am I going to do this?" And maybe the first ten seconds. After that, thirty minutes is easy.

Stop picking up your priorities one at a time to see if they fit. Manage them like you would a puzzle!

Write it down, organize, schedule, and execute. Bam! Your puzzle is complete!

39

ROTATING CHIVE

Feedback is the breakfast of champions.
—KEN BLANCHARD

THIS ONE IS a little embarrassing to share, but worse for the other guy.

Years ago, I was meeting with a potential client over lunch at a Perkins restaurant. This was a guy I met with a few times but never did much business. I don't know what I ordered, but I know for sure what he ordered, a salad, probably Caesar. As we were sitting there eating and chatting, I noticed he had a pretty healthy-sized dark-green chive on his front tooth. Nice. What to do? Well, I figured I'd just keep the conversation going and hope that little sucker disappeared.

What actually happened was that it kind of rotated around that tooth between his talking and chewing but never actually left. It just hung on, taunting me, challenging me to call it out.

I went to the restroom. The hope was that he'd keep eating and eventually flush out Mr. Chive. As I headed back, I was praying it would be gone. But if not, I was desperately trying to decide whether or not to tell him.

I sat down. And there it was, full circle from its last post. Yeesh. It was clearly determined. I should tell him. Man, I don't want to.

I didn't. This was fifteen years ago. It's probably still there.

My friend used to say, "If I had something in my nose, you'd tell me, right?" My wife says, "You'd have my back, right?" I do.

If it were a closer friend or family member, I think I'd talk. I probably should have in the latter case as well. Mostly, it's me. I don't want to feel embarrassed by something that's likely embarrassing to him. It's kind of self-centered on my part.

What are we not telling people that they need to hear? What if that guy had a huge client presentation after our lunch meeting? Yikes, I've never really considered that. But I have been better about feedback since then, any kind of feedback, the gross ones like this example and the more important ones about relationships, commitment, integrity, and habits. It's part of what I do. I'm also more receptive to hearing it. Assuming it's from a trusted source, feedback provides an opportunity to grow through our blind spots.

How about you? Would you have called out the rotating chive? Do you need to be more forthright with others and more receptive to good feedback for yourself?

40

SAVE THE SPIDERS

Love and compassion are necessities, not luxuries.
Without them humanity cannot survive.
—DALAI LAMA

OUR DAUGHTER, MADI, now twenty-six, loves snakes, bugs, and spiders. As a kid, Madi used to spend time outside picking up rocks, wood, and other things to find the bugs that might be hiding underneath. She often found, caught, and played with the biggest wolf spiders you've ever seen. She even taught her younger brother, Mitchell, now twenty-two, to be almost as comfortable with these little critters.

But her older sister, Brittany, now twenty-nine, never was interested in playing with spiders. It's not that she was afraid or repulsed, just not interested. A quick story about Britt shows that, despite not having her sister's love of spiders, this doesn't take away from her level of compassion, even with spiders.

One day recently, she saw a spider in the corner of the bathroom and just watched it for a little while. It just hung out, like spiders do. If this were my wife, she would have immediately run straight to me.

"Spider!" I won't say what my solution is since some of you may align with what I'll share about Brittany.

She wanted to catch it and take it outside. I can't tell you how many times she's done this. But being in the corner, she'd have killed it upon trying to catch it. She figured she'd just see where he was next time and left. He stayed right where he was for a few days. Then one day, he was gone. My wife would have lost it, her imagination soaring. She'd check her hair first and then come find me.

Britt just looked around a while, hoping it would be easier to catch and save in its new spot. But she never did find him. Maybe he'll come back; perhaps he's elsewhere. Maybe he's looking for my wife!

It occurred to me that Brittany has more compassion than I realized. She really did not want to kill this spider. She wouldn't necessarily begrudge others who do but just can't bring herself to take a life.

Mitchell took a homeless man to lunch and learned his story one day. Madi worked with autistic kids and is now in senior care. She has amazing compassion and patience for people with special needs. My wife and I sometimes grab a Little Caesar's pizza and drop it off to the homeless guy on the street corner. He gleams when we hand out a steaming box of pizza.

Do you need to be more compassionate? Does choosing to do something compassionate lead us to feel more compassionate? Even if we don't always feel it, maybe we should just do it, and the feeling will come. As Zig Ziglar said, "Act your way into feeling."

I need more of that compassion. Maybe I can learn by promising to catch and release spiders from now on. Except if they get away and Amy finds out, yeah, maybe I'll learn compassion another way.

41

SILENCE SPEAKS

*You cannot truly listen to anyone and do
anything else at the same time.*
—M. SCOTT PECK

EVER TRY TO stare down a dog? Not a challenge as eventually she'll get distracted or bored with looking at you. Ever try that with a cat? If you did, you may still be doing it because the cat doesn't look away. They're tough to stare down. It's almost creepy. I think they know the one who looks away is the one not in control.

Years ago, I had a manager with a very unique style of communication exemplified in certain strategic situations. I often tell this story as it teaches some great lessons. We would meet in his office to discuss ideas, strategies, sales, or simply something I wanted. Upon my presentation of ideas, I would pause, as is the common protocol of communication. (Ok, I'm done, your turn ...).

Then it got interesting. He would simply look at me (feeling like the cat stare) and ... nothing. After an eternal three-second pause, I'd start talking. He obviously needed more, right? And then I would stop. Remember, it was his turn now. Another stare and pause. And you guessed it, I'd start talking again. And so it would go. Inevitably, I'd leave the meeting not getting what I wanted and feeling like I had a lot less credibility than I had coming in!

After several of these engagements, I decided to change my approach. I walked into his office, sat down, shared my thoughts, and then shut my mouth! He stared; I stared. He continued staring. I began sweating (in a Cool Hand Luke sort of way, of course) but continued staring.

This is absolutely true! Finally after thirty minutes (probably more like ten long seconds, but it felt like a half hour), he spoke. And guess what? I usually walked out with my ideas accepted, more confidence, and ultimately more influence. Did I stare him down? No. What I did was mirror his communication.

Even though it was and still would be very uncomfortable for me, I adapted to his style and gained better communication and influence because of it. Was he staring me down? No. He was thinking, which translated into focus and silence. And guys like me don't really understand silence. We tend to think we must fill it, usually with us, usually not good.

Ultimately, I believe the relationship was far more effective when I learned to communicate in a style that worked for him and me. Let me also say that this is a wonderful individual for whom I have great respect. His communication was just different than mine, and I learned to recognize and embrace it.

I did, and we succeeded.

42

SPARKS MATTER

What we do for each other before marriage is no
indication of what we will do after marriage.
—Dr. Gary Chapman

CPR IS A well-known acronym for cardiopulmonary resuscitation. And most of us from my generation learned it in health class. Anyone remember that? Thankfully, I have not had to apply it, though I did the Heimlich on my daughter twice. One time, she was turning blue! Fortunately, I went two for two! Praise God!

Since I have not used CPR on a real human being and have not practiced it in forty years, I may be rusty. I experienced enough medical shows to have seen it over and over, but I should probably brush up on it. In the best case, I should learn it again.

CPR saves lives. No question. And it saves marriages, too. No question.

Early on in our marriage, my wife came up with a concept to help our marriage thrive. She calls it CPR. And it works in a very different yet no less effective way. CPR for marriage stands for compromise, pursuit, and respect. Be deliberate and effective with each of these, and you'll be a long way toward a long and immensely fulfilling marriage.

Most of us married people practiced CPR before we put that ring on. We put our best selves out there. We compromised, we pursued—oh, did we pursue—and we respected. We couldn't get through the dating phase without them. Then dating turned to "I do," and some of us eventually didn't, not consistently. And it was not right away, but over time. I believe pursuit takes the biggest hit.

Pursuit takes effort and intention. Sometimes it takes faking it, but that only works if respect is present. We know it matters, but we don't feel it anymore. That's where Zig Ziglar's wisdom comes in. Sometimes you have to act your way into feeling. And that works.

You define pursuit. A couple should probably define it together. It's different for everybody. You might check out Gary Chapman's 1982 classic, *The Five Love Languages*, to find out how you feel most loved and how your spouse does.

You might consider building a mutual list. Each writes the ten things their spouse does that makes them feel loved and another five you'd like them to do more or add. Talk about an open-book test. You have the answers now! Let the chase begin.

A marriage without pursuit is like a birthday cake without candles. No candles, no fire. And what's a marriage without some fire?

43

**C
H
A
P
T
E
R**

STICKS AND STONES

Pay less attention to what men say. Just watch what they do.
—DALE CARNEGIE

STICKS AND STONES may break my bones, but words can never hurt me. What a crock!

Tell that to the thirteen-year-old girl who gets bullied over social media. Words. Or the seven-year-old Little Leaguer who can't get a hit while the coach's kid is the superstar. How's that feel when the other players are talking about what a loser he is? Words. What about the lunchroom conversation about a coworker's divorce. "Hey, did you hear …?" Words. Gossip is defined as "casual or unconstrained conversation or reports about other people, typically involving details that are not confirmed as being true." Words. Always negative.

I recently heard Darren Hardy tell the following story. I found it online at www.moralstories.org.

> *Once upon a time, an old man spread rumors that his neighbor was a thief. As a result, the young man was arrested. Days later, the young man was proven*

innocent. After being released, the man felt humiliated as he walked to his home. He sued the old man for wrongly accusing him.

In court, the old man told the Judge, "They were just comments, and they didn't harm anyone." The judge, before passing sentence on the case, told the old man, "Write all the things you said about him on a piece of paper. Cut them up, and on the way home, throw the pieces of paper out. Tomorrow, come back to hear the sentence."

The next day, the Judge told the old man, "Before receiving the sentence, you will have to go out and gather all the pieces of paper that you threw out yesterday." The old man said, "I can't do that! The wind must have spread them, and I don't know where to find them."

The Judge then replied, "The same way simple comments may destroy the honor of a man to such an extent that one is not able to fix it." The old man realized his mistake and asked for forgiveness.

Sticks and stones might hurt your bones, but words might destroy you. Words matter, especially your own.

44

TAKERS, TRADERS, AND INVESTORS

No one has ever become poor by giving.
—ANNE FRANK

YEARS AGO, I heard a highly successful businessman tell a story about his leadership journey and how one statement from his dad completely changed his success pathway. This man was in business with his dad, building an organization of leaders for personal and professional development. They would hold meetings at regular intervals to share their business ideas with potential leaders who might join their mission. He would only attend those meetings when he had something personal to gain, like growing his organization by those he invited. If he had no one personally attending, he would not show.

Eventually his dad pulled him aside and simply told him, "You are a taker." How would you like to hear that from your dad, particularly if you're part of his business?

In a recent audio, I heard the speaker share something similar but broke it out further. He said people tended to fall into three categories:

1. Takers. These people do what the label says and what the man referenced above was doing. They take. They do not give. They show up to receive. They speak to be heard. It's about them and them alone.

2. Traders. These people give *conditionally*. Traders try to fool us and sometimes themselves. They will help, but only if it will be reciprocated. Some are outright about it; others just keep score, and trust me, payment will be required eventually. Interestingly, I'd prefer a taker over a trader. At least takers are clear about their interest.

3. Investors. These people give and often receive; they just don't plan or make *receiving* the condition. In a way, the lack of return is a gift in itself. They're investing in the relationship, the cause, the opportunity. The mere definition suggests there will be a return, but that return or the level of return is not guaranteed. These are the unconditional, unselfish leaders you want in your organization and life. The best marriages are built with investors. The best businesses are made up of investors. The best teams thrive with investors.

This year, let's commit to being investors. Let's give and give again. Let's invest in people, even ourselves. Let's invest in our marriage, kids, teams, community, and church. Let's not keep score.

After hearing Anne Beiler of Aunt Annie's Pretzels speak at a local leadership event, I remember one thing that stuck with me, "Give, to receive, to give again." That pretty much nails the investor mindset.

45

THE BLUE VASE

*America was not built on fear. America was built
on courage, on imagination and an unbeatable
determination to do the job at hand.*
—HARRY S. TRUMAN

CHECK OUT A little but powerful book called *The Go Getter*.
I hope you know the story, but if not … Cappy Ricks owns an old
lumber company and is vetting his latest recruit, Bill Peck. This new
employee, Peck, exceeds expectations and gains the attention of his
mentor and leader, Cappy Ricks. With this, he is given an opportunity
to prove himself, though he is unaware this is a test as he goes about
the task given to him. This is a seemingly simple and personal task for
Cappy Ricks. Go and purchase a blue vase for his mentor's upcoming
wedding. Simple, not really, as details are left out and answers are
unavailable due to Cappy's strange disappearance.

Peck is on his own and must show dogged determination, tenacity,
and passion for hunting down this blue vase. Through numerous and
intense obstacles and challenges, he finds the blue vase, a task that
most everyone would fall short of completing.

Another small book, a classic called *A Message to Garcia* by Elbert Hubbard, carries a similar theme. Once again, purpose, honor, and loyalty drive the delivery of a critical, life-saving message to the absurdly hard-to-find Garcia. The blue vase mentality shines through with the little-known officer (Rowen), who delivers the message against all odds.

I love these stories and the lessons they drive home! The message in each must be taught to today's generation. If only more people really grasped the value of these timeless attributes of leadership and success: determination, tenacity, drive, focus, and loyalty!

What is your blue vase?

46

TIME CONFETTI

*The choices that are most powerful in generating
motivation, in other words, are decisions that do
two things: They convince us we're in control and
they endow our actions with larger meaning.*
—CHARLES DUHIGG, *SMARTER FASTER BETTER*

HOW MANY OF you have seen "New Year's Rocking Eve" with Ryan Seacrest? Can you picture it? The ball drops as Ryan counts us down, "Five, four, three, two, one … Happy New Year!"

And then there's the confetti. Quick research says it's over three thousand pounds! That's one-and-a-half tons of tiny paper strips floating all out in front of us. If you're in it, you can't see through it.

A few months ago, I heard an interesting analogy to confetti. Picture all the tasks you do, you don't do, and you think about doing. All the distractions in between, the emails—oh, the emails—the texts, notifications, and junk phone calls are everywhere. And what about those thousands of random thoughts? Let's not even go there!

Imagine every piece of confetti in front of you: those you have to do, didn't do, others want you to do, and probably something you shouldn't do. Urgent!

I've read that one distraction can cost as much as ten minutes lost, sometimes much more. Five distractions in a thirty-minute task equals one hour and twenty minutes! Can you relate? Plus, the thirty minutes within the hour and twenty are far less effective than the thirty minutes with no distractions.

Think about your day. How much of what you do has your full presence for any real duration of time? And not just at work. What about your spouse, kids, parents, and friends? Yikes!

Time confetti is unproductive, draining, stressful, and unhealthy. It's time to clear the confetti and work with focus, presence, and stuff that confetti into boxes you choose to open only when you're ready. You'll get a lot of the right stuff done in less time with better results.

What's important?

- Work: key projects, strategic thinking, and people
- Home: your spouse, family, you time, and sleep

Let's turn all that time confetti into neat little boxes, tight compartments of focused energy, attention, and effort. Stephen Covey calls these boxes the "big rocks."

Let's save confetti for its proper place with Ryan at New Year's!

47

TIME FOR A LITTLE YOU TIME

*Own Your Morning will guide you to create personalized
daily rituals that center you, energize you, and give
you the power to fully show up for your day.*
—JAY SHETTY

IF YOU'VE EVER taken a flight, you'll know this drill. The flight attendant instructs us that in case of emergency and the oxygen masks drop, immediately put them on your kids or others who are struggling first. That way, those less able are saved by those more able.

Right? Wrong! Those who are less able will not be served by us because we might just be incapacitated before we get to them! We're instructed to first put our masks on and then help others. It's counterintuitive and yet lifesaving.

You can't help others unless you help yourself first. That's a tough lesson, one that most people should heed, not just in an airplane but in life. And it's not about being selfish. It is about being self-less.

What do we want for those we care about: health, growth, great relationships, security, adventure, loyalty, and connection? And what are we doing to develop those key areas in our lives? It's about you time.

One great way to get a little you time is in the morning. Some call it the morning routine. Although not for everyone, most mornings are the best predictable, least distracted time of the day. Sorry for those of you raising babies! Hang on, the time will come.

The morning routine is you time.

- Time to exercise: build your health, energy, strength, and vitality
- Time to read or listen: educate and grow your mind in all areas of importance
- Time for devotions or meditation: slowing down for spiritual growth

I do all of this in about seventy-five minutes every weekday.

And it's easy if you have a little discipline up front with a solid system you follow daily. Remove barriers. Stop snoozing. Put out your exercise clothes the night before and in your way in the morning. Have the coffee ready. Put a book out or have a podcast ready to go.

After a few weeks, you don't even have to decide anymore. There you go, you time.

48

TIRED OR UNINSPIRED?

*When we start a new task or confront an unpleasant
chore, we should take a moment to ask ourselves "why."*
—CHARLES DUHIGG

A COUPLE OF weeks ago, my wife and I were enjoying some time together at our fire pit. Our son pulled up after a hard but successful day at work. He always takes time to come over and talk with us when we're at the fire pit. So he came over, said "hello," and then proceeded to tell us how tired and beat he was and that he had to head in, grab some quick food, and drop into bed. Done.

This guy is highly animated and incredibly conversational. He loves to tell stories and make people, especially his mom, laugh. And he does all that, but not this time. He was clearly wasted (not drunk).

But then I asked him if he'd quickly show Mom the video he took of me completing a very difficult climbing route at the gym. This was one he set as a specific challenge for me, and I finished it earlier that day. He was proud of the set, and he was proud of me. He's a great coach.

Well, what a transformation! Mitch became a new man. He was now animated, charismatic, expressive, and engaging. He told other climbing stories and stories from work and hung out with us for another twenty or thirty minutes.

What changed? Was he really tired or just uninspired? Climbing is one of his top passions. He'll never be uninspired when talking about that.

Nobody really likes being tired unless it's time to sleep. My longtime friend and mentor used to tell me, "Mike, when it's time to sleep, sleep. When it's time to be awake, be awake. Don't confuse the two."

If you're tired but it's not time to sleep, shift your focus, take a controlled break, disrupt your mindset, go for a walk, stretch, and call your spouse, anything that inspires you. And that will carry you through.

49

TO BE SEEN

*Any fool can criticize, complain, and condemn—
and most fools do. But it takes character and self-
control to be understanding and forgiving.*
—DALE CARNEGIE

OH, TO BE seen! I've always had the luxury of coming home from work, opening the door, and getting an immediate and enthusiastic welcome from my wife and kids. My wife always won, but the kids were right there, greeting me like they hadn't seen me in weeks every workday.

Then years later, it was my dogs. And yes, my wife still beat them back to get to me. The kids, meh … And now, no kids. And the dogs, well, meh …

Now Emmett, our almost-four-year-old grandson, and my wife race to welcome me. Yes, she lets him win, and yes, she's still right behind him. We're hoping this goes on for a long time with many grandchildren yet to come.

The one common denominator is my wife. She always shows up. She makes me feel like the most important person in the room. And I know there are just two of us! Oh, to be seen!

Have you ever been to a family event with a distant relative, a community event for the first time, or a business networking event? You walk in alone, not knowing anyone. You see the circles of people, and the primal fear of not being accepted immediately spikes, how to breach the circle without that sense of being the outsider.

Then someone sees you and nods. That's all it takes. You're in. You're welcome. You're accepted. Oh, to be seen!

We need to do that more, to be the one who nods, the one who offers what we all need when coming home, meeting a new group of people, or joining a new workplace, to be validated, accepted. Do we do this when onboarding a new employee or client? Did we do this with our spouse, and are we still doing it?

We're all leaders. We have influence, with or without the title. And if you're an effective leader, you'll recognize and honor one of the greatest human needs, to be seen.

50

TRASHY HABITS

Change might not be fast, and it isn't always easy. But
with time and effort, almost any habit can be reshaped.
—CHARLES DUHIGG

I'M NOT A fan of any trash in my car. Nope. Can't stand it. But I do love coffee, especially Starbucks, anything bold. And I like to save money, too.

Several years ago, Starbucks had a promotion that if you bring in an empty bag of Starbucks coffee grounds to any of their retail stores, you'd get a free coffee. I'm in!

So after we finished our weekly bag of coffee, I grabbed the Starbucks bag and put it in the car. I intended to bring it in for that next free coffee, probably tomorrow, a good plan.

Only I didn't get to a Starbucks for weeks. But through those weeks, I had that nasty, irritating bag of coffee, garbage, still in my car. Finally, the occasion arose to stop at Starbucks for a little work time on the road. It was perfect. I'd stop in, trade my trash for my free coffee, and then settle in for some quality work time.

I got out with my garbage in hand, happy to have it out of the car, and promptly dropped it in the trash container just outside the store. I walked in, ready for my free cup, only to realize I had just tossed it! Well, at least it wasn't in my car anymore. I paid for my coffee and pondered my mindless mistake. And I never saved another Starbucks coffee bag again.

According to Charles Duhigg in his book, *The Power of Habit*, we make 40 percent of our decisions every day out of pure habit. We don't think about it; we just do it. My habit was a clean car. It's not a bad habit, but it superseded my intention of the free coffee. I didn't think about it; I just did it.

In some ways, that's good, but in so many others, it's not. Money habits, gossip habits, health habits, nutrition habits, listening habits, and confrontational habits are subconsciously executed. The question is whether they're productive or not. And if not, it's time to change, which takes a deliberate, proactive mindset.

Choose habits wisely! I lost a free coffee and, worse, carried around a bag of garbage in my car for nothing!

51

WHAT WE THINK ABOUT

Action cures fear.
—Dr. David Schwartz

IN OCTOBER 2001, I was attending a regional sales meeting. It was a month after 9/11, and I was with a group of salespeople discussing the impact of the aftermath on our sales. Most people were talking negatively, very pessimistic, and sharing expectations of a downward spiral in sales. There was nothing they could do, as customers surely were not open to new ideas or working with new providers. Yes, we'd just have to hunker down for a while.

Well, that was not my attitude. I figured this was the time to keep connecting, to keep being proactive and building upon positive expectations. When times get tough, leaders step up. They run toward the storm and push through. I did that in 2001, and my book of business continued to grow.

That sounds a lot like what we're experiencing now, April 3, 2020. Granted, this pandemic is unprecedented; we're navigating waters we've never experienced before. But what are most people doing? They're feeding the negative, pessimistic side of their imagination.

None of us really knows how this will all eventually play out. The news is questionable, often contradictory, and incredibly dynamic. The only thing in our control is how we think and what we do with what we think.

Take action. Take precautions. Be smart. Be safe and careful. But don't stop adding value. Add value to clients by serving them any way you can. Add value to your family by making the most of the increased time together. Add value to yourself by listening to and getting around smart, positive, and proactive thinkers and working on some of those big projects you've wanted to get to. And get outside and exercise. Fresh air, sun, and outdoors, what a great treatment for boredom and anxiety.

Some great mantras I've heard along the way may help you rethink what is happening and what we can do about it.

- "We become what we think about most of the time." *What are you thinking?*
- "Beliefs drive behaviors." *If you believe you will lose, you will act in accordance with that belief and make it so.*
- "Action cures fear." *What actions can you take to proactively navigate success right now?*
- "We move in the direction of our most dominant thought." *What thoughts have been filling your mind and driving your actions?*

Some of us will come out of this worse than we started, and others will come out better. What we have to understand is that it is a choice. What do you choose?

52

A MILLION LITTLE CUTS

I must govern the clock, not be governed by it.
—GOLDA MEIR

CHAMPIONS DON'T DO extraordinary things. They do ordinary things, but they do them without thinking, making them too fast for the other team to react. They follow the habits they've learned.

Years ago, I wrote an article called "Ten Speed Time Management." The concept was based on the metaphor of biking in tenth gear, consistently and effortlessly, until we hit the city. There we find people, crosswalks, cars, stop signs, animals, streetlights, and even garbage. All are obstacles that impede our progress and speed. We have to shift down to the lower gears, shift up, and then down again, never getting close to tenth gear and moving far less efficiently.

Isn't that what our day often looks like? That's the metaphor— schedule top priorities, known as "big rocks"—in tenth gear. Get rid of all distractions and stay fully focused. Your kids, your spouse, and your health need tenth gear. Let the low gears handle the little, urgent stuff so there's always room for the bigger picture. Ride most of your day in tenth gear. It's much more fulfilling, energizing, and fun.

I'd like to dig deeper into those distractions. They seem relatively harmless: checking that text, taking a quick call, and, of course, the coup de grâce of cuts, email. We're checking email incessantly, literally hundreds of times a day. Let's not forget the social media drug, and hey, how about news and sports? Did COVID get anyone's attention?

Constant distractions and interruptions are killing our productivity, blowing up our anxiety, and stressing us out. They're like a million little cuts. You don't notice them until it's too late.

Big cuts are painful and obvious. But those nasty little cuts are cutting away our time from what's really important. It's time to pay attention.

What little cuts are killing your top priorities?

ENJOYED THESE TIME OUTS?

If you would like to receive these 60 Second Time Outs directly to your inbox every other week, sign up for free at www. integrityworkscoaching.com - click on "Sign up for our newsletter".

HOW CAN MIKE SERVE YOU OR YOUR TEAM?

Speaking—Inspirational keynote speaking/teaching or team training on soft skills growth - leadership, communication, goal setting and accomplishment, sales, time management, and team building.

Coaching—One-on-one, in person or virtual coaching on leadership, sales or life. Build the person before you build your business, team, role, and life.

HOW CAN I CONNECT?

Email: mike@integrityworkscoaching.com
Phone: 717-226-4306
Twitter: @Greenecoach
Facebook: IntegrityWorks Coaching
Linked In: www.linkedin.com/in/mikegreene66

For more information about available services please visit - www.integrityworkscoaching.com

Printed in the United States
by Baker & Taylor Publisher Services

Printed in the United States
by Baker & Taylor Publisher Services